WHY I LEFT CHURCH TO FIND JESUS

A Personal Odyssey

Julie McVey

Published by Strong Oak Press, CA

Why I Left Church to Find Jesus: A Personal Odyssey
Copyright © 2019 by Julie McVey. All Rights Reserved.

Cover designed by Pezhouse Graphics

Julie McVey
Visit my website www.julieview.com

Printed in the United States of America
First Printing: Nov 2019

ISBN 978-16713975-7-6

To my children, Austin and Alex

Parenting changed me.
As a parent, I began to understand God
through the eyes of a parent rather than
through the eyes of a confused and fearful
child; and it was ultimately through that
humbling and transformative experience as a
parent that God finally made sense to me. Not
the unpredictable and scary God that my
church taught me about but the loving and
compassionate God of Jesus that my heart
taught me about. There is nothing a parent
would not do for their children. Love never
gives up. And there is no fear in love.
I have been so blessed to be your parent.

Julie McVey

ACKNOWLEDGEMENTS

Thank you to my husband who has been my biggest source of support for over 32 years. Thank you to my children who taught me a depth of love I had never quite known before. Thank you to my extended family and dear friends, both near and far, who continue to love me for who I am no matter where my path is leading me on this crazy and wonderful spiritual journey. I truly appreciate all the love and support I have received in my life.

Julie McVey

INTRODUCTION

I wrote this odyssey as a snapshot of some of my most challenging and even ugly religious experiences in a fundamentalist megachurch in an effort to more fully embrace breaking free from an unhealthy authoritarian religious indoctrination and to process the grief that emerges from the religious shunning that sadly, but often inevitably, results from this kind of religious deconstruction. Christians, ex-Christians, and religious outcasts will relate to the heartache, confusion, and betrayal of not only a religion lost but, more painfully, of friendships lost. Such loss is often the catalyst for a much needed spiritual transformation and great healing, which is the fortunate outcome of this particular journey.

Julie McVey

CONTENTS

Julie McVey

ENTRY ONE: *SPARE THE ROD; SPOIL THE CHILD*

"To spank or not to spank, that is the question." You all know what play that line comes from, right? Just kidding. I am so glad we are past that stage in our parenting. Our sons are 18 and 21, but I remember when I had my first child and that was *the* topic of the day for us new moms in my Bible teaching fundamentalist church. I mean it's all there in black and white: "He who spares the rod hates his child" (Proverbs 13:24). It couldn't be more clear, right? In fact, every topic we needed direction on in life was right there in our "How To" manual, otherwise known as the Bible.

I remember experiencing that warm feeling of inclusion when I was invited to a moms' gathering at the home of the pastor and his wife. My first son was only a few months old. Their little girl was older than my son. She was already sitting up and eating solid food in her highchair. But when the little girl would not eat her food properly, she would get a sharp flick to the side of her mouth by her mommy. We moms would be assured, "That's the only way she'll learn to eat her food properly. You have to apply a small amount of pain right at the moment of disobedience." I remember thinking, "But she's only a baby. Is this really necessary? I know I've seen people use this kind of training on dogs, but...? Well, this is the pastor's wife and she's definitely holy; I've heard her pray and she knows what she's doing, so maybe I should consider this with my baby."

I came to find out that there were a couple books going around in Christian circles at that time called, *On Becoming Babywise* and *Growing Kids God's Way*. I was strongly urged to purchase these books, so I could raise my children in a more godly way. The books are written by Christians, so naturally we Christian moms were to blindly accept them as authoritative guidance for raising our children. Apparently, *Babywise* is currently the only parenting book being sold that the

American Academy of Pediatrics (AAP) has said is unsafe to babies. Shockingly, these books are still being sold *and even* used today.

> In fact, every topic we needed direction on in life was right there in our "How To" manual, otherwise known as the Bible.

As both a new mom and a new Christian, this was one of my earliest memories of righteous training, so to speak, from a woman of God. A couple decades later, this woman of God would send me a letter of dismissal, not only as a sister in Christ but as a friend.

(Featured artwork *Mother and Child* by Carolyn Anderson)

ENTRY TWO: *MUSIC TO MY EARS*

Auditioning for the praise and worship team was a positive experience. The worship leader was a kind, encouraging, and musically talented man married to a lovely woman who was also very musically gifted. My favorite part of the whole church experience was worshipping with these uplifting people. At that time, the praise team was full of joy and heartfelt expression. I instantly felt a connection to my soulful sister ("in Christ") who not only had a beautiful voice but a huge heart. She took me under her wing and simply loved on me and encouraged me to be Spirit-filled and Spirit-led in my expression during worship. What a wonderful and fulfilling time that was. There was no other time during my church involvement I felt so connected to God and to others. And, to be frank, I had very little Bible knowledge then. I just trusted the love of others, the caring relationships, and the joy in the moment.

As in any church, worship leaders would come and go. I remember being under the leadership of one who said I needed to take it down a notch and be less Spirit-filled. I found that odd. Later, another worship leader came along who was quite different from the rest. After several years on the team, I had taken a break but wanted to come back to "my roots" and use my gift of singing once again as an opportunity to give of my time and connect with others. After some interviewing by the new, young worship leader, he was not convinced I was dedicated enough to the Lord to be on the team. The reason? The church had implemented a new requirement, of sorts, where one had to be associated with a community group in order to be considered qualified to serve at the church (at least, for some volunteer positions); and my husband

and I were not in a community group at that time. Apparently, we were not quite Christian enough to volunteer, and I was disqualified for consideration to participate on the worship team. Who knew that being in a community group was a biblical requirement to volunteer and serve in church? That was a new one.

> *Apparently, we were not quite Christian enough to volunteer, and I was disqualified for consideration to participate on the worship team.*

I did try to connect through giving of my time in other ways, but it never felt the same after that. Oh how I missed the days with my soulful sister in Christ (who had passed away by then) and that feeling of unconditional love, of my old worship pastor who recognized I had a gift to share, and of just loving the Lord as the Spirit filled me and led me. But those days were gone...and to be honest, I did truly miss it all.

(Featured artwork *Radiant Light* by Erin Hanson)

ENTRY THREE: *TONGUES, HEALINGS & DEMONS, OH MY!*

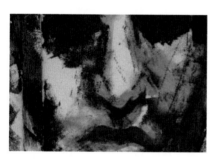

I guess I should backtrack a bit. One of my earliest experiences with Christianity was when I was 16 years old, after I had just moved out of my mom's house. My mother and father had been divorced for two years. Long story, but let's just say I grew up in a dysfunctional household. The day I moved out, my mother and I had been arguing all day. I went up to the patio roof to tan, or should I say bake? Many of you will remember the 1980s with its baby oil for tanning and lemon juice in the hair for lightening. My mom was screaming at me, and I was so pumped up with adrenaline I leapt from the patio roof—without injuring myself—packed my car with all my things, and drove off to live with my friend and her family.

I lived with my friend for only a short time, but while there I met a young woman who "introduced me to Christ" and shared the Good News with me. She brought me to her church, but I found it all a bit strange with the laying on of hands and falling down in the aisle. I was told they were "slain in the Spirit." I tried to keep an open mind, because I was so moved by that story they told me of how this Christ loved me so much that he died for me. I certainly needed a little unconditional love at that time in my life. My new friend was insistent that I had to "speak in tongues" to be assured of my salvation. Of course, this new demand on me seemed a bit inconsistent with the idea of unconditional love, but I was not going to argue. I wanted what these people had—community, relationship, love.

I was not quite sure how to speak in this strange new tongue, so I agreed to go with my friend to a church retreat where I would learn to speak this new language. The retreat was quite lovely. Everyone was kind and caring. During prayer circle, they kept telling me to just open my mouth and allow words to flow out without trying to form intelligible words. Well, that sounded a bit like humming to me, so I just did it. Everyone was so thrilled. I guess that was my initiation into their club.

> *It would be more than a decade later that I would find my church—the place where I would...learn the hard truth that a few charismatic requirements were the least of my worries when it came to pleasing God and being assured of my salvation.*

As much as I felt connected to the beautiful story of the love of God in Christ Jesus, that church experience did not last long. All the "charismatic requirements" never resonated with me. It would be more than a decade later that I would find my church—the place where I would be baptized, make close friends, be on the worship team, raise my kids, and learn the hard truth that a few charismatic requirements were the least of my worries when it came to pleasing God and being assured of my salvation.

(Featured artwork by Emre Can)

ENTRY FOUR: *MISSION POSSIBLE*

Sunday used to be church day but not any longer. I miss the community feeling of it all, but I don't miss the guilt trips from the podium. I remember one friend expressing to me that she often felt kind of icky after a sermon, because our pastor was so good at reminding us of how sinful we were and how far we had to go to be pure and set apart before a holy God. We often left church feeling like our dad had just shamed us for not being a good enough kid. "Why can't you be more like your brother, Jesus?" Surprisingly, many years later she would be one of the women who sent me a letter of dismissal as a friend and sister in Christ due to my current "heretical" doctrinal positions. Apparently, the positions I hold taint my character and disqualify me as a child of God.

I took it as the "Gospel Truth" the first time I heard our pastor speak of eternal conscious torment. He was the one with all the education, after all. And, let's face it, it's not that difficult to say, "God, please forgive me for my sins. I want Jesus, whom you resurrected, as my personal Lord and Savior." As long as you "declare with your mouth that Jesus is Lord and believe in your heart that God raised him from the dead, you will be saved" (Romans 10:9). A "ticket to Paradise" and out of the grips of hellfire took one simple, public confession. It's plainly stated and is so simple a child could do it. Of course, if a child did *not* do this, that child would spend an eternity away from God in conscious torment.

> *As the thought of billions of souls rotting away in eternal conscious torment sank in, I began to realize that this was urgent.*

The other doctrine that was slipped into all this is *predestination*—the idea that God picks and chooses before the foundation of the world who will be able to make such a confession. As easy as it is to say this simple salvific prayer, billions *would not be able* to because they simply were not among "the chosen" before the foundation of the world. For whatever reason—the feeling of belonging, trust in the pastor, that so many intelligent people accepted this as the truth—I did not put all the puzzle pieces together until much later to make the connection that *we were worshipping one horribly violent and sadistic god.*

As the thought of billions of souls rotting away in eternal conscious torment sank in, I began to realize that this was urgent. It didn't really occur to me at the time that if everyone was predestined one way or the other, what was the need for urgency? All I knew is that I needed to begin taking this *very* seriously and save my family and friends before the Rapture. The Rapture, as many of you know, is another doctrine taught where at the end of this wicked age of human history, the Lord Jesus will remove all believers from the earth and allow the wicked to wreak havoc on the earth for a few years. During this time, the Lord will give the rest of the "chosen ones" time to come to their senses and repent before Jesus takes a torch to the planet.

And so, my evangelistic efforts began. I had a wonderful sense of belonging with a friendly community and a mission to save souls from an eternity of suffering.

(Featured artwork *Redwoods* by Erin Hanson)

ENTRY FIVE: *THE BEGINNING OF THE END*

This entry is a tough one for me because of the personal nature of it. It is something that was so very hurtful in many ways. In the last entry, you see that I began my genuine evangelistic efforts to save the world. I trusted the Bible, and I trusted my pastor and my church to uplift goodness and to be just. Let me backtrack again so you get a bigger picture.

My father and mother tried to conceive and failed over and over again. By the time I was born, my parents had adopted a girl and then a boy and were ready to adopt another. I was the third adopted. I was brought home within hours of my birth. A little over two years later, my little sister was born to my father and mother who had never conceived together before and would never conceive together again. She was a wonderful gift! I shared a bedroom with my sister all my years growing up, until I moved out in my late teens. I sure love my little sis!

Unfortunately, my sister had more medical difficulties than the norm. I desired to protect her. Of course, I was only a child myself. In some ways, she gave me a purpose: to look out for another besides myself. For various reasons, she had some self-esteem issues. She met a boy in a Christian Bible study group. He pushed for marriage even though she was only 17 and he was 21. After knowing one another for only a few months, they got married.

Because she chose to marry as a minor, she had to put herself through college rather than get financial help from our father. Her husband injured his back early on in their marriage and could not help much with the finances. My sister worked, pursued a bachelor's degree, and then went on to get a master's. During this time, her husband stayed home with their two boys. In order to protect the privacy of my sister's family I will not go into details here, but her husband got himself into a great deal of trouble with the law and was arrested on multiple occasions. His bail ended up being a difficult financial burden for them. More distressing than that, the children were greatly impacted by their father's indiscretions. My sister and her husband went to counseling at the church. Her husband repented. She was expected to forgive him, as if she hadn't already done so over and over again during their decade plus of marriage. She later discovered that he was still engaging in lawless behavior, and she was simply done trying to trust him. She finally divorced him. The church made her feel like the one in the wrong, because she chose to divorce him without "biblical grounds."

> *As I look back on my experience with how the church handled this, I realize now that this was the beginning of the end.*

It wasn't long before they gave her ex-husband a job doing camera work for the church. My husband and I discovered this when the recording crew arrived at our house to film us for a marriage series they were producing. I couldn't understand why they would give him this particular job knowing the details of his struggles and all the problems this had caused him and his family. When I saw him I was speechless with shock. I had to pull myself together and do this taping.

My husband and I shared our concerns with the church, but we never felt they were taken seriously. In the end, my sister was pushed out and made to feel like a horrible sinner and her ex-husband was embraced. As I look back on my experience with how the church handled this, I realize now that this was the beginning of the end.

(Featured artwork *The Tear* by David Mcaree)

ENTRY SIX: *CALLING EVIL GOOD AND GOOD EVIL*

Our church had no problem calling out certain sins and parading the sinners in front of our megachurch congregation before either allowing them to stay among the "true believers" upon genuine repentance or "delivering the sinner to Satan for the destruction of the flesh" (1 Corinthians 5:5); if they did not repent according to the terms of the church leadership. After the treatment of my sister and her situation with her husband and marriage, I should not have been surprised by this next public display of a very private matter.

There was gossip about one of the younger married pastors having some kind of inappropriate affair with one of the girls from his youth ministry. Our senior pastor read some email in front of the entire congregation about how this youth pastor did not "go all the way" and *just* had continuous flirtations through texting and private meetings with the young woman. The gossip was already spreading, and I wasn't sure how sharing this email in front of thousands of people did anything but make things worse.

This news did inspire me to research what exactly the Bible said about divorce, with and without "biblical grounds." The talk was that since he did not actually engage in sexual intercourse with the young woman, his wife was *not allowed* to divorce him without being in sin. They went to church counseling and the wife tried very hard to put the pieces back together again. It was eventually discovered that the husband continued in his flirtations and texting even after counseling. That turned out to be far too many pieces to put back together, and divorce became inevitable. I reached out to the wife, because I felt heartbroken for all she was going through and wanted her to know that not everyone in our church felt she was wrong or a bad person for considering divorcing this guy who hurt her *over and over* again and who she could no longer trust with her heart.

At the suggestion of a good friend, I purchased a book about the topic of divorce to help me navigate through these uncharted waters. It's called, *Divorce and Remarriage in the Bible: The Social and Literary Context* by David Instone-Brewer. I also bought a copy for the senior pastor and left it for him at his office, but I never heard back that he received it, let alone read it.

> *Something was not sitting right with me when it seemed the victim ended up in the wrong and was cast out, but the abuser—since he supposedly repented— remained in the church with nearly a victim status.*

Long story short, the husband remained a member of the church and the wife was shunned. After years of giving of her time and resources to the church and developing some very close relationships, she lost most of her dear friends from the church and was made out to be the sinner in the situation. She is now in a loving marriage and continues to have very strong faith, but at the time it was devastating for her.

It was real life situations like these that led me to buckle down and want to know what the Bible really had to say about these kinds of things. Something was not sitting right with me when it seemed the victim ended up in the wrong and was cast out, but the abuser—since he supposedly repented—remained in the church with nearly a victim status. I began to dig into Scripture more and more to help me understand how to make sense of all this.

(Featured artwork *Bitten Apple* by Scott Conary)

ENTRY SEVEN: *THE END IS NEAR AND ALL IS WELL*

Let's get into the thick of it, or should I say when I was in the thick of it— the time when I was reading and studying Scripture several hours a day. Yes, you read that right! I spent many hours a day in Scripture. After all, I was not only on a mission to save souls, I was determined to understand what the Bible really said about the more troublesome doctrines we Christians were expected to believe. But a few years before this time, in my early days of being a Christian, I didn't get much out of the Bible. It didn't make a whole lot of sense to me. I could not seem to connect the historical or even the spiritual dots, so to speak.

What I did love was the *Left Behind Series*. I was addicted to those books! I became fascinated with eschatology, and I took some classes at our church led by teachers who would later be included on the staff at a college now known as Eternity Bible College. I could see how easily the Book of Revelation could play out as written in the *Left Behind* books, but I was more drawn to these fictional books than the Bible and that concerned me. I prayed and prayed that God would give me as much passion for the Bible as I had for these books. My training was that a good Christian devotes time to not only prayer and going to church on Sunday but spending time reading Scripture.

Well, several months later, as I just mentioned, I was happily spending several hours a day in Scripture devouring and memorizing all these amazing historical stories, Messianic prophecies, and eschatological realities. During this time, I still believed in eternal conscious torment, a Calvinistic theology and, of course, the Tribulation and the Rapture. Anyone who has adhered to these beliefs will empathize with the sense of urgency I felt in regards to the salvation of all the many lost souls out in the world. I remember sending out a mass email to friends and family regarding the end of all things that was certainly imminent. Everything I read in the news made it clear that the end was near. I was disappointed to later learn that some of these friends and family members thought I had jumped off the deep end, and they were concerned for my emotional and psychological well-being. I did not hold it against these misguided souls who didn't know what I knew. I knew Scripture, and the Bible *plainly revealed* that in the last days these things would take place. Not only that, but my pastor and my educators, who had degrees in theology, said the same thing. These people weren't crazy. They were well-educated, intelligent people. They would not mislead anyone. They loved people and wanted them to be saved. Surely, I could trust them.

> *...when my final conclusions led me away from some of those shared beliefs, it didn't take long before I was known as "deceived, misled, and giving in to the ear-tickling desires of worldly ways."*

When Facebook came out, I eventually created a Bible group. It was a long time before I even created a Facebook account. I am a bit slow to move in the area of technology. I held onto my flip phone for as long as

I could. I upgraded only when it became clear that the younger generation was moving into texting, and my flip phone did not have convenient capabilities for that. Anyway, I began a Facebook Bible group, and I guess I created a bit of a reputation for myself. Many began coming to me for biblical advice. Some came to me through the group and some would simply call me up and ask. I remember a sermon our pastor gave, and he got onto some theological subject and finally pointed me out and said, "Look, I'm not as well educated in this as Julie here. Just ask her if you need more information on it."

When I believed all the same things as my pastor and elders believed, I was highly respected. In my theology classes, the instructors seemed to really enjoy all my questions and pushback. However, when my final conclusions led me away from some of those shared beliefs, it didn't take long before I was known as "deceived, misled, and giving in to the ear-tickling desires of worldly ways." But that came later. At this point, I was enjoying the worship team, Bible reading, the respect of my mentors and pastor, and the many friendships I had developed through this church community. Life was good.

(Featured artwork *Reaching Out* by Gail Sawatzky)

ENTRY EIGHT: *LOVE DOESN'T WIN*

 As I pondered how the church handled marital trials and divorce, it seemed that they readily forgave the transgressor and unjustly condemned the victim. Nevertheless, I convinced myself that, surely, the church was taking what they felt was the most biblically sound approach. Even if the church leadership neglected the divorce debates of Jesus' day as background material that would enlighten interpretation, (as I had learned about in the book I mentioned previously), they were doing their best to remain consistent and true to Scripture. They had good intentions. And, most importantly, that did not put a stop to my evangelistic efforts. After all, the possibility of people burning in Hell was at stake. Not only that, but I learned of the Rapture, which was certainly imminent. Jesus was

about to come out of the sky and take up all the true believers and leave all the fake believers and non-believers on earth to go through the most catastrophic time the world had ever seen. I spent many nights weeping on my knees in prayer over all this. My heart was broken for all that was going to come upon the earth.

> *It certainly was tempting to listen to someone who thought all could be saved and that love would win in the end, but that was just a temptation of the flesh.*

I remember when Rob Bell's book, *Love Wins*, came out. Our pastor and very good friend warned us against this heresy, and I stayed away from it, of course. I did not want to be one of those who just went after teachers who taught what my itching ears wanted to hear. It certainly was tempting to listen to someone who thought all could be saved and that love would win in the end, but that was just a temptation of the flesh. Eventually, our pastor wrote a book of his own in response to this alleged heretical teaching.

As I shared the Good News of the Gospel (to accept Jesus' invitation to be saved from Hell and enter Heaven after death, i.e. fire insurance), I continued to study Scripture. During my studies, I came upon many inconsistencies regarding the teaching of eternal conscious torment, and it was not long before I moved on to the belief of annihilationism. This is the belief that after final judgment, those who do not believe in Jesus as Lord and Savior will be totally and completely destroyed. Perhaps some punishment first for not figuring out the right things to believe about God before death, but not endlessly tormented. This doctrine was not only more sustainable with Scripture, it seemed much more humane than eternal conscious torment. I felt a sense of relief to recognize that my God was not so bad after all. At least He did not torture people endlessly for not believing in Him and bowing down to worship Him. He just snuffed them out. That sounded much more merciful. Thank goodness. And to top it off, the co-author with my pastor of the response to Rob Bell's book changed his view to annihilationism as well. That was a surprise to me, and I thought I must be on the right track. After all, this was a scholar who knew a lot more than I did in my simple studies. Of course, I came to his same view before I knew he did, but that did not matter—*God was not so bad after all*, and I felt a sense of relief in that.

But, still, I guess this meant that love doesn't win, at least not for all humanity, and I eventually had to come to terms with that.

(Featured artwork *No Paradise* by Nik Helbig)

ENTRY NINE: *LOSING GOD IN MY RELIGION*

It is time to backtrack a bit once again. I shared my formal introduction to the Gospel of Christ and my first memorable experiences with a church setting when I was 16 years old, but I did not share my first experiences with God. After "coming to know Christ" through the Gospel, I used to wonder to myself if I would have never known God and never been saved if I had never been introduced to the Gospel. After all, aren't we commissioned to share the Gospel so that people can come to know God through Christ and be saved?

I grew up in a family where my mother had Catholic leanings and my father had Protestant leanings, but neither really raised us children in either religion. We were not churchgoers, we did not read the Bible, and there was little to no emphasis on God at all. There was basic prayer before supper and simple prayer at bedtime. That was the extent of my knowledge of God. Now that my siblings are grown, I would describe my older sister as agnostic, my older brother as atheist, and my younger sister as evangelical with both fundamentalist and charismatic influences. Each sibling took a bit of a different path, but I do not think it was our religious upbringing (or lack thereof) that influenced our direction.

The thing I find interesting is that even though there was little to no religion taught in our home, and even less spirituality emphasized, I found myself to be a very spiritual child. I cannot remember a time when I did not contemplate the spiritual or think about God. I remember praying fervently as a young child nearly every evening. I pondered about God throughout my day. I would wonder who this Being was and what our grand purpose was all about. I would wonder about the unseen parts of reality (or non-physical) and how they interacted with the visible parts of reality. I was fascinated with the miraculous and angels and how the spiritual dimension could possibly intervene with the physical dimension. I would often gaze up into the mysterious night sky or sometimes stand on the beach peering out into the vast ocean on a dark night and feel the very presence of God and know deep within me that we are so much more than what meets the eye.

What led me to be convinced that there was a spiritual existence of some sort, even as a young child? Looking back, it seems I innately perceived a spiritual realm. I did not need to be convinced; it was simply how I perceived reality. My fundamentalist teachings would tell me that this was nothing more than me acknowledging general revelation as described in Romans 1, but it was more than just acknowledging God's existence. I talked to God. I sensed the presence of God that was sometimes nearly palpable. I knew God, maybe even better than I knew God after "coming to know Christ" through the Gospel, through church, and through Bible study. I guess it depends on what one means by "know." Sure, I learned about the history of Israel, the story of Christ, and the growth of the first century church, but did that knowledge improve my connection with God? Was this information even necessary to have a connection with God?

> *After years of "growing in the grace and knowledge of the Lord," I began to miss God.*

After I became a Christian, the more Bible knowledge I accumulated, the more the image and perception I had of God *shrank*; and this magnificent Divine Being eventually became quite different from the delightfully mysterious and wondrous benevolent One I had perceived in my childhood. I figured it was all part of the process and that my theological studies would answer burning questions that would lead me closer to God. But it only left me disillusioned and more confused, and somewhere along the way I lost my carefree, childlike faith within the complicated maze of a well-studied mind. *After years of "growing in the grace and knowledge of the Lord," I began to miss God.*

(Featured artwork *Kiawah Drama* by Rick Reinert)

ENTRY TEN: *SOMEWHERE OVER THE LGBTQ RAINBOW*

The time during my thirties through my early forties is filled with some of my most cherished memories. I was in a great place with the church community and with church friends. As a stay-at-home mom and on-and-off homeschooler, I got to spend loads of time with my two growing boys who made me laugh and cry and want to pull my hair out and want to go to the moon and back to see them thrive.

I also appreciated the time I had to indulge in my theological studies. Some might say I have a bit of an analytical mind with more of an academic bent, so studying Scripture in an intense and thorough way allowed me to fill that need to have my mind engaged in something mentally stimulating. As I studied over the years, more and more fundamentalist doctrines began to fall apart with critical analysis. I studied everything from the Trinity to the theodicy of God to the doctrine of predestination to the doctrine of Hell to the doctrine of End Times, and the list goes on. I suppose I remained in good standing with the church and my church friends, because none of these doctrines are considered particularly salvific in nature. Of course, when I implied that there was biblical reason to have hope in universal reconciliation, that is where I crossed the line, but I was not quite there yet at this time in my life. The first doctrines to fall apart for me were the Calvinist doctrine of predestination and the doctrine of the traditional Hell. Those were easy to debunk, in my opinion. The futurist doctrine of End Times took much longer for me to deconstruct, partly because I was deeply entrenched in that particular doctrine. I had previously invested a lot of years studying it and defending it, and it seemed my eyes could see only a futurist view of Scripture for the longest time.

It wasn't until I participated in an online study of what the Bible says about homosexuality that I began to lose the respect of some of my church friends as a "true Christian." The study was facilitated by a well-respected scholar who happened to be non-affirming, but he did a thorough study with the group and provided evidence for both a non-affirming view as well as an affirming view. He was not as convinced by the affirming view. He remained non-affirming, and I think he still is at the time of this writing. Anyway, I publicly posted what I was learning each week and asked questions as a way to work out the tangles in my own mind as I was researching. In the early stages, everyone seemed on board with going through such a study. Some of my friends chimed in and asked questions, commented, or encouraged me and the process I was taking. As time went on and I was honest with my personal findings, I began receiving more and more heated and even angry comments. After it was all said and done, I landed firmly on the side of affirming. I was no longer persuaded that the Bible condemned gay love, intimacy, and marriage. As the months went on, I continued to educate myself with the LGBTQ community. I learned many things, but one thing especially began to crystallize in my heart: *I'd rather stand before God and Him tell me I loved too much and that my love clouded my judgment than Him tell me I didn't love enough and that my judgment clouded my love.*

This affirming view, along with my more inclusive view of reconciliation that came later, was the position that abruptly ended my standing as a "sister in Christ" with some of my friends. Some of these friends were those with whom I had raised my children over the past sixteen years and with whom we enjoyed many family vacations. These were not just acquaintances; these were people with whom we had invested years of love and friendship. Now all that was *simply erased* due to the cultic, religious mandate that Christians who cross arbitrary doctrinal lines shall be shunned and excommunicated as a form of discipline that is designed to coerce them back into a particular way of thinking.

> I'd rather stand before God and Him tell me I loved too much and that my love clouded my judgment than Him tell me I didn't love enough and that my judgment clouded my love.

Ironically, it was this "discipline for my own good" that has led me to never want to step foot in church again, at least not that kind of church. I was still open to exposing myself *and my kids* to that line of teaching by going to church, until my Christian friends produced the ugly fruit of longtime exposure to such teaching. That utterly shocking treatment ended any possibility of me returning to church. This, of course, is the opposite of what they intended for me. In their misunderstanding of Scripture, they wrongly think that this type of treatment is somehow justified by Matthew 18:15-20, which relates to when a Christian directly sins against another Christian and shows no sign of remorse for the harm they have done. It is understandable that one would want to distance themselves from such a person—a person who has done or continues to do them harm and has no intentions of changing their behavior. Sadly, they and many other shunning Christians misuse this verse to excuse carelessly writing off relationships over doctrine. In doing so, they create a barrier much like the barrier that Christ is said to have torn down between the Jews and the Gentiles: "For he himself is our peace, who has made the two groups one and has destroyed the barrier, the dividing wall of hostility" (Ephesians 2:14).

All is well, though, because there are plenty of inclusive churches where love, rather than control, is the driving force and the message is: "There is neither Jew nor Gentile, neither slave nor free, nor is there male and female, for you are all one in Christ Jesus" (Galatians 3:28). I am thankful for the LGBTQ rainbow that led me to churches where *wings are not clipped through fear and condemnation*; and freedom in Christ, through the driving force of grace and love, *allows the spirit to take flight and "soar on wings like eagles"* (Isaiah 40:31).

(Featured artwork *Happy* by Itay Magen)

ENTRY ELEVEN: *UNFAILING LOVE*

 Not only did the doctrine of eternal conscious torment go up in flames after a bit of careful study, I never did come to terms with the idea that a loving, merciful God would simply snuff out people who didn't figure out all the right things to believe about God before they died. This doctrine still struck me as lacking. What about people who never heard the Gospel of Christ? What about people who lived peaceful, loving lives out of the conviction of their hearts but never felt the need to make any kind of public confession regarding Christ? What about mentally and physically broken people who continually made poor and even harmful choices in their lifetime, but had they been born into another body or another environment would have lived an entirely different kind of life?

> *How is it just to annihilate a human being for not figuring out the right things to believe about God before death?*

As I researched and asked questions, some Christians suggested I was emphasizing God's love *over* God's justice in order to make God more palatable. But many of those same Christians believed that if one said the sinner's prayer right before death, they would go straight to Heaven. The thief on the cross is a good example of this. He confessed his sin just before his last breath and was assured a place in Paradise. What about the thief on the other side of Jesus? God's mercy runs out after one's last breath? What about the millions of Jews who died in the Holocaust? Did they go straight from the horrors of a gas chamber to the horrors of a fire pit? How is it just to annihilate a human being for not figuring out the right things to believe about God before death? All these questions and more were swimming in my head as I researched.

Although the doctrine of annihilation is sustainable with Scripture, there are also Scriptures that give support for the doctrine of universalism. It was the story of the Prodigal Son and the experience of being a parent that finally tipped the balance leading me to land on what some refer to as "the doctrine of relentless love." What was it about the father of the prodigal son that made the father never give up? *I think it's love*...relentless, unfailing love. "Love never gives up, never loses faith, is always hopeful, and endures through every circumstance" (1 Corinthians 13:7). Does God's love give up after one takes their last breath or does love never give up?

Ironically, recognizing and acknowledging this relentless and powerfully transformative love of God would be the impetus for some of my closest Christian friends to give up on me and walk away from our friendship. I could either reject the idea that God's love is relentless and receive the conditional love of my friends or I could embrace the idea that God's love is relentless and endure the rejection of my friends.

(Featured artwork *Endless Freedom* by Willem Haenraets)

ENTRY TWELVE: *THE RESURRECTION OF THE BUNNY*

I was looking back through some old pictures today trying to find a couple shots of the boys when they were little on Easter Sunday. It was one of the two biggest holiday celebrations in our home all through the years.

There was a time when I was going through a stage in my theological studies when I decided I needed to rethink celebrating a holiday with pagan roots. I had always showered the boys with Easter fun, including painting eggs, Easter baskets on Sunday morning, and of course, hunting for the colorful eggs left by the Easter Bunny. I began to feel like I was taking away from Jesus and his glorious resurrection if I made Jesus' day all about a special Bunny, painted eggs, and yummy candy.

I compromised and decided I would still include some Easter fun but make certain the boys knew that this was really "Resurrection Day" and not Easter Day. They were older, but they were still children and I did not want to just abruptly stop Easter as they had always known it. One year I created a little treasure hunt for them with hints left around the house that led them to different hidden gifts. The hints included messages that were not only clues to find the next gift but messages relating to Passover and the Resurrection. Looking back now, I am so glad I did not rob my kids of a little magical time just because I was going through another "theological stage."

> It is still too painful for me, even if it is Easter Sunday. That building still represents the place where some of my closest friends put religion over decades of friendship.

At the time of this writing, it's Easter Sunday. We are doing something completely different today. We are not going to church. It is still too painful for me, even if it is Easter Sunday. That building still represents the place where some of my closest friends put religion over decades of friendship. We are not cooking and having a big celebration with family and friends. I am simply not in the mood to celebrate in that way. I want to go back to simpler times.

Last night, the Easter Bunny stopped by and left goodies and hid Easter eggs for my adult boys to discover. It may sound silly, but do we ever outgrow the simple pleasures of a little innocent magic? That is what I need today. Some childlike magic. Just my family. Just my kids. Back to when it was simple and pure and easy. A time when the Easter Bunny was the only threat to Jesus' day. A time before it became clear that the real threat to Jesus' day is religiosity and its followers.

So, it is time to resurrect the Easter Bunny and all the childlike, innocent magic that it brings. Happy Easter!

(Featured artwork *Posse* by Rebecca Haines)

ENTRY THIRTEEN: *GOD*
LOOKS LIKE JESUS

Going through the often long and arduous process of critically analyzing various doctrines, many of which are assumed to be "Gospel Truth," was what it took for me to make my way slowly to the light at the end of the tunnel. I am *not* saying for one moment that I have it all figured out. I am just saying that there is definitely *more light* where I am now than where I began. I was in a dark place. Not always, but often. I wept for all the lost souls and for the horror to come at the end of the world, and for what people would go through when the "God of wrath" would rain down his retributive fire on those who got it wrong. *I literally wept.* My eyes would be so swollen the next day that I could barely see out of them.

> *Out of all the doctrines I evaluated, there was one conclusion that made all the difference in the world to me: God looks like Jesus.*

Out of all the doctrines I evaluated, there was *one conclusion* that made all the difference in the world to me: *God looks like Jesus.* Now, that may sound obvious, but to voice that and to truly internalize that is the difference between looking at a delicious meal when you are famished and hoping it will satisfy you and actually feasting upon that meal and enjoying every bite as it fills both your deep inner hunger and your intense desire to taste all that is good. I am sure many in my old church would *say* that God looks like Jesus, but they are still starving. When faced with the internal struggles of cognitive dissonance that comes from believing in an all-loving, self-sacrificial God who dies for His enemies but is coming back to smite them with retributive violence and throw them in everlasting punishment; it leaves the hungry, searching soul famished for that which it was created: *the unconditional and restorative love of the Divine.* "The Spirit and the bride say, 'Come!' Let the one who hears say, 'Come!' And let the one who is thirsty come; let the one who desires take the water of life without price" (Revelation 22:17).

For me, God looks like Jesus, and when I see Jesus, I see a lover of my soul. My first memory of this lover of my soul was that tangible presence of comfort when I was a child. As a teen, it was that intuition telling me that love is not found in unintelligible language and fits of emotional fervor. As a first-time mom, it was that still, small voice telling me that I did not have to spank my baby to fit in. It was the beauty found in the music when I worshipped and still find in all kinds of music to this day. It is the compassion and empathy that swells within me as I recognize the injustices in the world and the sorrows of those suffering. It is the self-sacrificial, unconditional, relentless love I have for my children. The lover of my soul *is pure light and radiates onto all as I allow it to be released* during this human experience of mine, for I am convinced that "God is light and in Him is no darkness at all" (1 John 1:5).

(Featured artwork *Release* by Steven Daluz)

ENTRY FOURTEEN: *THE DAY MY FRIENDS WALKED AWAY*

Speaking of darkness, the months leading up to the 2016 presidential election were certainly dark and challenging. I slowly began to see things in the Evangelical community that I could no longer justify. I was truly shocked at the blatant hypocrisy. Before this time, I shared rather tame posts on social media, like family pictures and uplifting quotes. I certainly posted theological questions, but most of my social media friends were on the same page as me, so there was not too much disagreement going on. As the presidential election neared, I became more and more concerned and did my best to share valid articles to help us all make informed decisions. I was not expecting the extreme polarization that would ensue.

It was also during this time I became more vocal about my LGBTQ affirming position as a Christian. I'm sure my posts began to look more and more progressive and maybe even, gasp, liberal. So, maybe it was a perfect storm brewing that would lead to my friends ghosting me and some outright rejecting me with their more formal letters of dismissal. I did recognize a bit of a disconnect with a couple friends and I understood it, but I would *never* just completely abandon a long-term friendship that was built on so many memories over a difference of opinion on religious doctrine or political views. I am a super transparent friend. They saw I was going through some changes. They saw that I had some internal struggles. Rather than be there for me even if they did not agree with my views, or even just allow some break time between us if they felt so disconnected, they simply cut off all communication with me.

This entry is by far the most difficult one for me to write. I am truly not sure how much to share and how much to keep private. My one longtime friend was the pastor's wife. We were not as close as I was with our other two mutual friends for various reasons, but we had spent many years on the worship team together and many weekends hanging out together. We were close enough that when her oldest daughter graduated from high school, she asked me to write her a graduation advice letter that is often written to loved ones moving on into the world. Understandably, when they all moved to Northern California, we didn't keep a strong connection. I remember the day we were uninvited to their oldest daughter's wedding. I had gone to the bridal shower, which was lovely. My husband and I had bought the airline tickets for the wedding. And, then, during a phone conversation our previous pastor and longtime friend told my husband that we *should not come*. The reason he gave my husband? They had *heard* that I was sharing views that were against what he preached, and his daughter felt uncomfortable about it. So, we didn't go.

Months later, I called a mutual friend of ours to catch up, but to my shock she suddenly interrupted me to announce that she could no longer have any contact with me due to my LGBTQ affirming position and my more inclusive approach to reconciliation. Unfortunately, our conversation was very brief as I had an event to attend. I was a bit startled by her unexpected rejection. We had been good friends for over 15 years. So, I reached out to our mutual friend, the pastor's wife, since I figured she not only had insight into our friendship but would *certainly* be a voice of unity. The opposite happened. She eventually wrote me back and said she believed I was "deceived by the devil" and "stirring up division" by voicing my opposing views in a public way, walking away from biblical doctrines and thus "walking away from my first love," and no longer a "sister in Christ." A few days later, I received a letter with suspiciously similar wording from our mutual friend. Rejected by another dear friend over doctrinal differences. I can only assume I had been a topic of conversation all along. Of course, I responded to each of my friends in an attempt to meet face-to-face to talk things out. I've never heard back from any of them. At the time of this writing, that was over a year ago.

I want to add something else here. Although this treatment by very close friends was truly shocking and heartbreaking, I was also quite disillusioned by the complete lack of support from other people from our church who knew us. I came to find out that several people knew about this "excommunication" and never bothered to reach out to me to say, "That's wrong" or "Sorry that happened to you." Reminds me of the words of Martin Luther King Jr., "In the end, we will remember not the words of our enemies but the silence of our friends."

The day my friends walked away was painful. I suppose it wasn't really "a day" but perhaps more of a process, but it *did not* have to be that way at all. There is no reason to end connection altogether, especially without warning or any kind of closure whatsoever. What a sad religion that encourages people to put doctrine over relationships. In essence, this act of shunning is pretending that another person has ceased to exist. While that in itself is painful, what the shunners may not realize is that *they force someone else to go through the loss of a person who's still alive.* The grief is real. It is a cruel and abusive practice still alive and well in many churches.

> *I was beginning to truly internalize that God transcends the boundaries of religion and any wall put up by that religion would eventually be torn down by the reconciling love of Christ.*

The day my friends walked away wrecked me. It ripped a hole in my heart. It was also a wake-up call.

It was a definitive sign that my intuition, the Spirit of God within, was right all along. Jesus, whom I had come to know as the expression and manifestation of the Infinite Source, was not bound within the walls of some church building and certainly not dependent upon some small group of friends I met in the short 80 years I would live out my human experience on this planet we call Earth. I was beginning to truly internalize that *God transcends the boundaries of religion and any wall put up by that religion would eventually be torn down by the reconciling love of Christ.*

(Featured artwork *You Ditch It All to Stay Alive a Thousand Kisses Deep* by Paul Lovering)

ENTRY FIFTEEN: *WHERE TO GO FROM HERE*

Where to go from here? Forward. I know I can't go back. I realize that now. Not back to those lost friendships. Not back to the church that excludes those who should be included. Not back to the theology that is driven more by fear and control than love and humility. I began writing this odyssey in an effort to receive some healing that can come through the process of simply writing an experience out. It has helped me to sort through the stages of how I came to certain places in my "religious life" and where the road took unexpected turns in my journey. Healing has begun here. That is not to say all the hurt is gone. It was hard enough to transition through one way of thinking about God and theology to another, but to be dismissed and rejected so easily by loved ones is a level of mistreatment that, sadly, many must endure to be true to where the Spirit of God is leading them in these more restrictive churches that do not respect or encourage free and independent thinking. I know the typical fundamentalist Christian would say one cannot trust one's heart or conscience or intuition. I would say these are the very conduits through which the Spirit of God leads us throughout our lives.

> *I wanted so badly to come to know Jesus better by studying the Bible, and it was through those years of study I came to recognize that Jesus gave a very different picture of God than the fundamentalist church did.*

I am not finished running this race. This brief narrative is just one small step of healing one small chunk (actually, a pretty good-sized chunk) of my life. But, as they say, all we go through is what makes us who we are. I know the title of this odyssey is why *I left church* to find Jesus, but in many ways the church also left me. *It abandoned me.* As soon as I had views that were far too inclusive, church people began distancing themselves from me. Eventually, even some of my closest friends ended up choosing doctrine over friendship, or any kind of connection at all. Sadly, the barbaric practice of shunning in the fundamentalist church is still used today.

I wanted so badly to come to know Jesus better by studying the Bible, and it was through those years of study I came to recognize that Jesus gave a very different picture of God than the fundamentalist church did. Where the church demands, "Be holy!" Jesus whispers, "Be with me." Where the church says, "Call out the sinner!" Jesus says, "Reach out to the broken." Where the church warns, "The path is narrow and few find it!" Jesus, the Shepherd, says, "Out of my one hundred sheep, I'll leave the ninety-nine to find the lost one." Where the church cries, "Vengeance belongs to God!" Jesus weeps, "Father, forgive them!" Where the church claims, "God's justice is not diminished by his love." Jesus says, "Divine love demands a justice that means victory for all, and all means all." In many ways, it's a matter of what one focuses on: the old or the new, the letter or the spirit, partial revelation or full revelation. In any case, for now we see through a glass, darkly (1 Corinthians 13:12); and being that's the case, our grace for one another should be abundant.

So, where to go from here? Wherever my path unfolds, I think I'll stick with the one I began this journey with in the first place, many years ago, as a child. *I think I'll stick with Jesus.*

(Featured artwork *Crystal Ranch* by Erin Hanson)

We shall not cease from exploration, and the end of all our exploring will be to arrive where we started and know the place for the first time.

—T.S. ELLIOT

ABOUT THE AUTHOR

I live with my loving husband, my two precious sons, and my two devoted dogs in sunny Southern California. I received a Master of Science degree from CSUN in 1999. I see myself as a fellow traveler among many on a transformational journey. My passions are family, relationships, creative awareness, and spiritual discoveries. I find writing to be therapeutic and a wonderful way to share my humanity, my heart, and my journey with others.

Made in the USA
Monee, IL
09 June 2021

70675869R10045